Blastphemy

The New Glossary of Golf

Words Every Golfer Needs to Know

Blastphemy

The New Glossary of Golf

Words Every Golfer Needs to Know

Tom Quarton and Bob Scher
Drawings by Peter Szasz

SunTam Publishing

SunTam Publishing, Inc.
P. O. Box 2610
Mill Valley, CA 94942
info@suntam.com

ISBN: 0-9787430-1-6
ISBN: 978-0-9787430-1-7
Library of Congress Control Number: 2006905984

To all who play this great game,
who will enjoy having the words
to describe the things that actually
happen—on every round.

From the Authors

In *Blastphemy, The New Glossary of Golf*, our aim was to fill a big gap. We've all been given golf, one of the greatest of all games, and our wonderful language. Yet where is the word to describe what happens when your ball, which has been careening to the right all day, suddenly — when attracted by a horrid pond — curves left, and falls in?

There was no word like *handicaptive* to describe the player (all too familiar) who gets into a sweat when his or her handicap *begins to shrink*. And where was the word we wished we had to describe a person who takes forever to line up a putt? Totally absent were the words to describe the specific feeling we get when were penalized by one of the many special rules of golf — like how to properly drop a ball after it falls into the pond — and there are no appropriate words to describe the flouting of those rules.

We've also included the inescapable *Laws of Golf Physics*, which could give physicists, who play serious golf, something to ponder.

We trust we have put an end to the frustration of the missing words and have given all of us, the players, words that we can recognize, remember, and *use*.

The Glossary belongs wherever players gather to discuss the wisdom and the mysteries of our game. We guarantee that you will find numerous occasions in almost every round to turn to it to clarify *what is actually happening*.

Bob and Tom

Naming What Actually Happens

Contents

SITUATIONS

Baffleball

The bounce or roll toward (or in) the hole that your opponent's ball always seems to get, and the bounce or roll away from (or out of) the hole that *your* ball always seems to get.

"Which is worse: *this*, or a broken heart."

Blastphemy

Curse words spoken immediately after failing to get out of a sand bunker.

"#%@&@**%#" is an example of blastphemy.

Clicksorrow

The sound of a golf ball hitting the cart path which implies that your ball has deflected to a remote location.

"All of my nightmares begin—or end—with that terrible sound."

Demonprint

A footprint left in a bunker. Your ball is in it.

"What's just as exasperating is that
these demons seem to enjoy their work."

Foralysis

When there is an actual need to shout, "Fore!,"
you are suddenly paralyzed and out of your
mouth comes nothing.

Geeces
(gee´-seez)

Familiar deposits left by geese into which your ball often lands.

"Ugh!"

Mistraculous
(rhymes with *miraculous*)

A miraculous shot at the wrong time—e.g., you've hit into the foursome ahead of you and they have (1) squished it or (2) driven it out of bounds or (3) promptly hit it back to you.

"A miracle—just when I could have done without one."

Mistraculous squared

A truly horrible situation as you have just made the drive of your life, but the ball sails *over* the foursome in front of you.

When confronted, you may find yourself saying, "I know nothing. It must have been the foursome *behind* us."

Nozone

The average human condition applied to the great game of golf.

"Ah, laddie, the *zone*—I know it exists. Old Tom Morris came to me in a dream."

Sandickery
(rhymes with *hickory*)

The preposterous notion that there is
something about a sand bunker that
prevents you from blasting out on your
first or second try.

"I wish I knew *why*, but that bunker on the
thirteenth hole has got me sandickered."

Shankenstein

Legendary monster who randomly dispenses the curse of shanking.

"Just before I shanked, I felt this terrible shadow moving over me. We are helpless mortals."

Slinker

An opponent's 20-foot or longer putt that rolls around the cup before dropping in.

"That proves that my opponent puts magnets in his golf balls."

Stumptser

A tree that stands in front of your ball.

"I love trees, and I'm a perfectly normal person. But this tree is *grinning* at me."

Troublockery
(rhymes with *mockery*)

The unreasonable effectiveness of a negative location to attract your ball, even though your ball usually goes the other way.

You are at the 11th hole and there is a dreadful pond to the left of the green. Your ball has landed on the right side of the fairway all day. You address the ball, you swing, and your ball drops into the pond.

But now you can say:

"It wasn't my fault. It was troublockery."

PEOPLE

Addzheimer's

A player's "affliction" that prevents him or her from properly adding up their score.

"What does adding have to do with actually playing golf?"

Blabbus

Someone who constantly verbalizes his rationalizations for his poor play.

"My new golf shoes are too tight so whenever I swing I feel I'm not able to really focus today. I got these shoes from a catalog that we usually keep on top of the refrigerator and I forgot it was there until last week, then I called up the company and talked to a real nice gal named Kim who said..."

Buckateer

A player who thinks the long game is the primary key to success. He spends hours every week on the range with buckets of balls. He spends little or no time working on his approach or putting.

"They keep telling me if I keep driving here, I'll break 100."

Cartiac

A maniac who drives his cart over fairways, greens, and possibly in front of you just when you're starting your downswing.

"I was meant to drive!"

Dragbagger

Someone who is always late for the game
and wastes a lot of everyone else's time looking
for his lost ball, and even finds original ways
to waste more time.

"I couldn't help being late. I forgot my golf clubs
and I had to go back and get them."

Foursome Prime Evil [FPE]

A dawdling foursome in front of you.

"I had never harbored a mean thought in my life until I encountered my first FPE. I wonder if there is a location in Hell where they have to play the 17th hole over and over again forever. And there's a jungle between the tee and the hole."

Gimmiepus

Someone who always takes a gimmie.

"It was a simple two-foot putt. Of course I took a gimmie. Saves time."

Curiously, a gimmiepus rarely consents to giving a gimmie.

Golfish

The restlessness and edginess that arises when an anticipated game is canceled for whatever reason.

"Sorry I snapped, Honey. But I'm golfish."

Golfwrath

The almost unbearable agony and anger that arise when two anticipated games are canceled in a row.

"Sorry we had a tiff, Honey. But I've got golfwrath."

Grippler

One who has too tight a grip.

"The tighter you clench, the more you will wrench."

Groker
(groh´-kuhr)

A very deep divot; also a player who frequently takes very deep divots.

"I can't explain this, but just as I was starting my downswing my club got longer."

Grunch Marks

Pitch marks left by uncaring **Grunches** or people who might become **Grunches**.

"Who wants to fiddle around with replacing ball marks."

Handicaptive

The strange malady that keeps players at their current handicaps.

"I really got scared after shooting that 40 on the front nine—but I got comfortable again on the back nine with my 52."

When a handicaptive's terror reaches psychotic proportions, they acquire

Beyondophobia

—the fear of permanently lowering their handicap.

Mechanosis
(me-kuh-noh´-sis)

The self-torture affliction that causes a player to try to recall, while driving, all of the mechanics required:

Before: "Is my chin up — arm straight — right knee *slightly* bent towards the target — early wrist cock—*both* wrists— ball correctly placed off left heel— left shoulder up?"

After: "I shanked, I shanked. But I know why! I fell back on my right side..."

A person who has mechanosis is a
Mechanoclastic
(rhymes with *plastic*)

Mumbledum

What a mechanoclastic who is also a Ph.D in physics says to himself while swinging:

"The lever force dilates the vertical vector so that the torsion involved is r over 43 times q squared..."

Outbounder

A player who never takes the stroke and distance penalty after hitting out of bounds.

"I assume when a ball goes out of bounds that it's no longer part of the game. So obviously there can't be a penalty."

Plutter

Someone who takes an infuriatingly long time to line up a putt.

An anthropologist observing a game:

"The head rolls forth and back, forth and back, when will it stop? The rest of the body is motionless. The other competitors are having difficulty resisting their violent impulses. This is an excruciating scene."

Sleemus

Someone who is unethical in play.

"It's just a game. Cool off."

Stormer

An opponent who is inexplicably immune to natural forces, such as windy days, rainy days, days full of hail, and worse.

The most renowned stormers hail from Ireland, Scotland—and West Texas.

" *'Blow, winds, and crack your cheeks! rage! blow!'* [*] Ha! Ha!"

[*] Courtesy of William Shakespeare, *King Lear, III, ii.*

RULES

Bagony
(rhymes with *agony*)

A penalty for having the wrong number of clubs in your bag.

Bagoner

Someone who consistently commits bagony.

"What's the big deal. I never use all these clubs, but I paid for them."

Clubdumb

You are penalized if you ask your opponent about club selection.

"I'm not asking you which club you used. But which one did you just put back?" (No go. The penalty stands.)

Debunkenbild

You incur a penalty for building a stance in the sand bunker.

"You try hitting this thing out of here without building a stance!"

Dream Dropping

There are numerous occasions where a player can opt to drop a ball. In these situations, you are not permitted to put spin on the ball or manipulate it in any way.

"But I had a dream last night that Ben Hogan told me that if I didn't put a spin on the ball it would be bad luck."

Stream Dropping

Dream dropping after landing in a water hazard.

"These hazards just get in the way of my game."

Dream dropping and stream dropping fall under the unfortunately large category of

Unplayable Lying.

Dumbledupe

When you hit your opponents' ball by mistake you incur a two-stroke penalty.

"But your ball was in a much better position."

Envirosmak

For bending or breaking tree branches, you incur a penalty. This is what happens to you when you are not *green*.

"Now trees are against me."

Frostration

You can remove ice from your ball (if it was made by humans) but not *frost*.

"So do you have to be actual chemist to play golf?"

Impedementia
(im-pe´-duh-men´-shee-uh)

In a bunker, you are not allowed to remove a "loose impediment," which is defined as any natural object such as leaves, twigs, stones, insects (living or dead), and MOUNDS MADE BY INSECTS. You may remove cans, condoms, money, etc.

"What about spiders? They're not insects. They're *arachnids*."

Knackler

An opponent who hovers over you, more concerned about catching you breaking a rule than playing the game.

Knackler: You removed a leaf in the bunker.

Player: The wind blew it away.

Knackler: You blew on it. Here's the photo and you look ridiculous. The penalty stands.

Life Relief–
Possibly *Your* Life

You are surrounded by wasps, an alligator, or any object that may want to eat you. You are permitted immanent relief from imminent danger. You may drop a ball.

Note. In 2005, fire ants were added to the imminent danger list.

"Ah! I can breathe easier now."

Long Lost Cost

A player spends more than five minutes looking for a ball. Penalty is stroke and distance.

"So it was seven minutes. Look, if I'm two minutes late for an appointment nobody minds. So what's the problem here?"

Poking Noser

You cannot ask your opponent about club
selection (see **Clubdumb**). But, amazingly
enough, you are allowed to look in your
opponent's bag to see which club is missing
(but you can't move or even touch anything
in the bag).

"Kindly get your snout out of my bag."

Walkwurst

If you hit your ball out of bounds or lose your ball, you must incur a one-stroke penalty plus *you have to return to where your played your last shot.*

This is the worst walk in golf—perhaps it is the worst walk in any sport.

"You cannot imagine my pain."

THE THREE LAWS
OF
GOLF PHYSICS

1) Newton's First Law of Golf:
$f = m/a$

Force does not always equal mass *times* acceleration. *The harder you swing, the shorter they fall.*

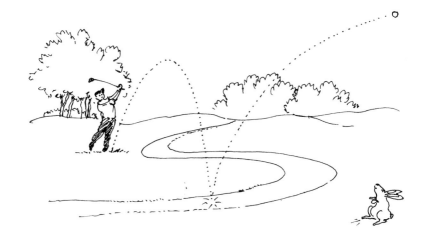

2) The Law of Rejection

This Law opposes The Law of Reflection, a law in ordinary physics. The Law of Rejection comes into play when a ball strikes something (like the cart path) and takes *an impossibly-directed bounce for an impossibly lengthy distance*.

3) The Law of Foreslay

When the word Fore! is employed, *a golf ball can go faster than the speed of sound.*

THE TWO GREAT
MYSTERIES
OF PUTTING

Elusivication
(il-oos´-i-vi-kay´-shun)

The ability of your putter to shift its sweet spot just as it is about to strike the ball. Also can be used to describe the result of a demon who substitutes bitter herbs for the sweet spot at the moment of striking.

"This is my fourteenth putter, and they have all had the same problem."

The green on which elusivication frequently occurs is sometimes called **The Elusian Fields**.

Shrinkophrenia

The closer you get to the hole the smaller it becomes.

"Now you see it; now you see it less."

This is especially true if your opponent has just sunk a 22-foot putt.

THE ONE
PRIMARY
GOLF OBSTACLE

Indesyzygy
(in´-des-siz´-i-gee)

Syzygy (a truly goofy word) is the straight-line configuration of three celestial bodies, such as the *sun*, *earth*, and *moon*, as in an eclipse.

Indesyzygy is the inability to line up the *target*, the *ball*, and the *clubface*.

It is a player's *indecision* when swinging, the opposite of *taking dead aim.*

Sightings

Date   Blastphemy Term   Name

Course   Notes

Notes

Date   Blastphemy Term   Name

Course   Notes

Notes

Date   Blastphemy Term   Name

Course   Notes

Notes

Date   Blastphemy Term   Name

Course   Notes

Notes

To send sightings to the Blastphemy website, go to *www.blastphemygolf.com* and click on *sightings*. Selected sightings will be posted on the website.

Date	Blastphemy Term	Name

Course	Notes

Notes	

Date	Blastphemy Term	Name

Course	Notes

Notes	

Date	Blastphemy Term	Name

Course	Notes

Notes	

Date	Blastphemy Term	Name

Course	Notes

Notes	

To send sightings to the Blastphemy website, go to *www.blastphemygolf.com* and click on *sightings*. Selected sightings will be posted on the website.

Date   Blastphemy Term   Name

Course   Notes

Notes

Date   Blastphemy Term   Name

Course   Notes

Notes

Date   Blastphemy Term   Name

Course   Notes

Notes

Date   Blastphemy Term   Name

Course   Notes

Notes

To send sightings to the Blastphemy website, go to *www.blastphemygolf.com* and click on *sightings*. Selected sightings will be posted on the website.

Index